PROVERBS FOR A WOMAN DRINKING ALONE

Talia Randall is a writer, performer and podcaster. Her work has been called "refreshing" (The Guardian), "sublime" (dig.com) and "distinctive" (The Upcoming). Talia has performed comedy, poetry and theatre on stages across the UK including Wales Millennium Centre, Southbank, Bristol Old Vic, Roundhouse, Glastonbury and the main stage at Larmer Tree festival. Talia's poetry has been published in the anthologies *Poems from a Green and Blue Planet* (Hachette Children's Group) and *Everything is going to be All Right* (Trapeze) as well as Bath Magg, Interpreter's House and Fenland Poetry Journal. Talia is also the creator of *What Words Are Ours?* a poetry knees-up that features Deaf and hearing artists on the same stage. Talia's BBC commissioned podcast - *Blossom Trees and Burnt Out Cars* - was released in July 2022 and explores who does and who doesn't have access to nature. Since 2007 Talia has worked with children and teenagers to develop their voices through drama and poetry.

ISBN: 978-1-915760-96-8

Cover designed by Aaron Kent

Edited & Typeset by Aaron Kent

Broken Sleep Books Ltd
Rhydwen
Talgarreg
Ceredigion
SA44 4HB

Broken Sleep Books Ltd
Fair View
St Georges Road
Cornwall
PL26 7YH

Contents

Proverbs for a Woman Drinking Alone

Talia Randall

For Tamir

The Aftermath

I thought my skin had come off
in one clean rip. A de-clothed
clementine, the peel
looking like an elephant's head
or cock and balls in my palm.

But I keep finding bits of skin
in places I'd neglected,
the soft passage
between shoulder and armpit,
the nook under my left bum cheek.

I strip them off.
Slide them between elegant glass panels.
Some look like Rorschach blots,
others like the Thames
from the credits to Eastenders.

I keep the catalogue in the garden shed,
exhibit them at summer get-togethers.
My guests clink flutes,
grill halloumi, lather me
with diplomatic applause.

five minutes before a shame

i hold my giblets
up to the light
see how ugly
the plastic bag is
bleach is the best filter
through which to examine
the greypink details
choke down
on a can of milk
is that dough i can smell
or a cherry flavoured condom
grip the plastic shower hose
orifices slimed with mildew
a mandatory splash of water
dishwasher warm
make a tent from a rubber glove
zip down the flaps
curl up quiet as a grub
small as a daughter

for the future museum

eat a spiralised dinner
watch the new adult Disney
sieve a bottle of diet pepsi
prepare the daily sock ceremony
count the doorslams
collect kirby grips from the carpet in lieu of a hobby
tell the printer to go fuck itself
pickle my scrolling thumb
ignore the scented candle
leave the house & tut loudly
reset a boomers gmail password
watch the london stadium fill up with bodies
sniff the oat milk for signs of life
call a social worker for Chip from Beauty & the Beast
high five everyone on twitter
respond to the text from Papa Johns
pretend to be the CEO of the frozen peas
forward the survey to five email contacts
fuck a houseplant
twos a bathbomb
how come my jaw won't open

January

Unusually horny
for this time of year
I fancy anyone
who calls their loved ones cunt.
I deliveroo a box of chicken,
save the skin to use as parchment,
everyone has a craft hobby nowadays
fermenting something jolly in the kitchen.

I flit between husky
ambition & stiff panic
from all the emptying lungs,
when I tune into K's funeral
her slot is double booked,
I refresh the live stream over & over
try not to eavesdrop
on someone else's ceremony.
Watch from bed.
Hold my pee tight in case I miss it.
Is that the same celebrant from Tee's funeral
20 years ago, in a wig
the colour of mushroom cuppa soup?
She's getting the pronunciations wrong again.
If I were a priest
I'd make sure to jot down the phonetic spellings
so I don't embarrass the dead.
Joni Mitchel, Randy Crawford, Terry Callier
sing bright through the sad tannoy.

Should I make a will?
Decide who'll inherit
my collection of sequin boleros.
The lump in my gut
is always there waiting
to be proved right.
Smug little cow.

The first lockdown babies
have been born.
I use up my vouchers
to send them little welcome gifts.

i am the lord of the dance said he is on a loop in my head at 5am

help / is there a childline
for grown ups
i'd like a bit of warm squash please
& can u spill
a little vodka in there thnx
help / can I use
marmite instead of miso
nevermind invite me round anyway
i'll bring a red & a white
& i can think of at least
six places to get valium
help / i think i've been using
the upside down emoji wrong
i am the lord
of the dance said he
is on a loop in my head
at 5am again

i want The Public to love me
i want an army of chubby girls
to meme me but
inside my skull there is nothing
but a naked bulb
a hissing fist
help / is that me
i can smell
or is the dog on the bed again

i'll go to the GP
watch her google my symptoms
i am lord of the dance
said he
is on a loop in my head at 5am
or is it 8am
if i say i'm running late
because the leccy ran out
do u think anyone
will believe me

The heroine

The men are in prosthetics
bold mustaches
expensive educations

there is one
woman alone
in the trailer surviving
on a diet of soup & shampoo

the stunt coordinator
can be seen in the frame
skulking behind the papier-mâché trees

the leading man forgets
he is meant to be
doing a spanish accent

a puppet will appear
voiced by a much loved comedian
who will one day
be accused of sexual harassment

the woman
female caucasian
innocent
busty
must be able
to play ages 19–21
convincingly
gets called on to shoot
her scene
gets taped over
by the yellow pages ad

I rip the film out the VHS
slot the video
between my thighs
clench & bury the remote in the back garden.

phil mitchell teaches me what a spleen is

man made of egg
unconscious in the pit
hooked up to a beeper
on an empty ward
its his spleen
they'll have to take it out

he sobs into the fire
flames lick the pram
quick take the baby from him
quick take his bottle
chuck his keys
down the plughole

another fight scene
& i'm on the foley stage
smashing wet celery
into broken bones
slapping beef skirt
for the *get outta my pub* finale

next episode he standstoops in a church hall
too much man
to use his eyes
hello my name is… and I am a…
biscuit crumbs for stubble
weak squash in a sugarglass tumbler

Curriculum

When we get to the bit about consent, I'm supposed to read from a laminated crib sheet. An educational film is meant to explain: a stick man makes tea for another stick man who doesn't want tea.

If tea = sex then what is a biscuit? If Sanjay, Miriam & David buy 3 apples for 50p how much change is left? If the Dish ran away with Mr. Hewitt after he got sacked for all the porn on his laptop then who is with the Spoon?

With the younger ones, I recite the P.A.N.T.S. rule, the acronym to remind them of basic bodily autonomy. *Everybody, say it with me!* *PRIVATES ARE PRIVATE! ALWAYS REMEMBER YOUR BODY BELONGS TO YOU! NO MEANS NO!* Etc

Who can define PRIVATES for me? I watch them, their failure to correctly name parts of their own bodies. I will them to say vagina or penis with the same nonchalance as elbow or earlobe.

In the staff room, an inspirational poster tells me I have to give myself permission, as if I were a schoolgirl politely asking to pee. *Let David go first, you girls can hold it in longer.* I thought David was busy buying apples?

All of life's lessons are taught in a single day: sex, drugs, how to write a CV, but in all the swapping of rooms & all the signing of forms no one bothered to ask the stickman what he actually wants. Does he know we're using him like this?

Later I will learn that shiner means blowjob

Damp with chips & choc-ices
we flop onto whatshisnames doorstep
Dya give shiners?
My lollipop face reddens
to meet his question.
We're experts at laying
traps, summer holiday landmines
full of slaps & piss-wet pants.
I don't know what shiner means
but I'm beginning to read
a new menace
growing in all the boys
& guess – *nah.*
whatshisname is a slab of
butter trying to chisel
himself into the men
who bulldoze his mother's woods.
He prods the other girl,
you a virgin?
She quivers a *no?*
then a feeble *yeah?*
& we shriek,
like feral cats that break
our sleep with their nightly racket,
fucking nature.
What do pussies do
with the barbed virility of the Toms?

Proverbs for a woman drinking alone

If a woman drinks
undisturbed in a forest,
does she even exist?

A man walks
into a bar,
and ruins the woman's evening.

If a woman never has to
hold her tongue
what does the cat get?

The man with the long face
thinks he's a gift horse,
he leads himself to drink.

Its reigning men
and a hard man is good to find,
find a keeper? Losers find her.

Make sex, not love,
better late than first thing in the morning
the early bird has worms.

Easy come, not so easy cum.
Remember, good things come
to those who masturbate.

Action man speaks louder than Barbie,
she shouldn't put all her eggs
in one basket,

unless she's considering freezing them.
The clocking bomb
of her biological time,

ticking every list
off her bucket
before she kicks it.

Keeping mum for later,
son is a bitch
like father, daddy issues

Self Care

I download a playlist of Sad Sexy Women™
with large guitars & kinkless hair
a hipflask full of Gaviscon at their belt buckles.
Some have hotglued glitter to the rim of their Stetsons.
In the bath I invent a private ASMR,
hone in on the intakes of breath
snatched between every "oh la la la"
legs tense in the bubbly water
the pruned skin of my index & middle fingers.

Under covers I indulge my obsession with Joan
from Mad Men. Brightness turned all the way up
I pinch the screen to asses her particular shade of lip,
the plum dress she wears in episode six.
I practice her walk at a party,
hold my pint like its a Brandy Alexander
& when another man explains
the real meaning of Fight Club, I quietly
remind myself of the true size of my clitoris.

My DNA test results are back –

58% banana.
I paid extra to learn that my allergies
might have an evolutionary function.
Well, sacrifice me to the pollen gods,
lay me on the altar!
Is that the golden calf
I can see or a chocolate bunny
wrapped in foil?

At the secret meeting
there was much debate
among the key stakeholders
on the best way to define ourselves,
58% banana, or 42% Other?
Or should we select 'other'
then in the blank space underneath
specify 'banana'?
Also, should we use capitals?
Also, where is our Capital?
I'm not allowed to speak (vagina)
so I nod & shrug
at the appropriate moments,
fist a pile of matza into my gob
chew it up into a sharp paste
to push around my cheeks.

Now that my spit is in G-d's database
I can never truly be off grid.
Don't tell my new comrades though
& they musn't know that I'm part banana,
not after all the trouble they went to

to make room for my campervan in the yard.
Every morning I do my best to blend in,
pray for a soul-patch to sprout
from my disobedient chin.
I would try joining them at beekeeping
but allergies.
When they speak to me at porridge-breakfast
I make my excuse to leave
'whoops I've left the genny on',
'I better go refill the waterbutt'.
Promise me you'll never tell them this
but every Monday I order a large cheese pizza
& swallow each piece whole like a lizard.

Dowry

The tablecloth was crocheted by
my mother's mother's mother's mother
in a plump lavender field,
in a long-forgotten
Europe between the wars.
'My dowry'

Safta left a coffee ring on it.
I remember it on the sideboard,
spread under a cigarette display case.
From nan I inherited
a tin of peaches
& a tin of custard.

They were still in date a year after
she died, I was going to make a trifle
on her birthday but found that dad
had eaten the syrupy fruit on a night
when he missed his mum,
spooning the juice like an airplane.

Bulgarian Rose Oil

the women in the rose fields
swap scratches cuts & calluses
for papery pink petals
the flower heads
musn't be bagged or they'll ferment
instead they are laid out
on the warehouse floor
like dead butterflies
& tipped into vats of boiling water
the sticky sweet steam
rises into metal pipes
four tones of roses
make one kilo of oil
one million six hundred thousand flowers
its worth more than gold

the grandmother cannot use it.
she keeps it in a wooden container
behind the glass
in a dustless display case.
every sun rise it evaporates
slowly wasted to the air
begs her *drip me onto your skin*

for lunch she chars a modest pepper
directly on the stove's flame
wraps it in a plastic bag
until the skin puckers
she only wants the fleshy inside
to mix with a little white cheese
yesterday's bread

on the daybed
she remembers the one
about the auntie
& the soiled white dress
on her wedding day
the boy who fell from the tree
after the ceremony
a hushed omen
folded into the family linen.
she naps,
dreams of turkish coffee
then the neighbour finds her
still in the kitchen living room
quiet while she sleeps
the tiles hear everything

Household

Father's beard is a swarm of bees.
Brother can't remember which teenage
mutant ninja turtle is which.
Sister builds an igloo out of choc-ices.
Mother pays for everything.

The stray cat visits & eats tuna
off the posh china.
Father calls the cat Jeremy.

Father sees himself in Jeremy.
Sister sees herself in brother.
Brother sees himself in the TV.
Mother realises she left
herself in the old country.

On the night they get cable
they invite the neighbours
round for a séance.

They rent the house from a giant
who sometimes thinks about eating them,
sometimes forgets they exist.

One day they buy it
with money,
they had run out of beans.

For breakfast they eat lard & avocado sandwiches,
& Jeremy does the weekly bills,
"too much on toilet-paper" he says.

Personal Statement

My teachers tell me I could really
Be Somebody, but instead of filling out
the form they gave me I dangle
my virginity from the window ledge
& make a performance of puffing on the hash
I swiped from dad's tobacco tin.

The neighbour boys hurry past
my window. They've aged sideways,
teens made men by too-soon babies.
I nod down to them, beg for one of them
to shoot me down like they used to
at least that way I'll know my place

but they're too busy grabbing nappies
from the shop at the edge of our estate.
The form asks me to explain myself
in 500 words (or less), but I can't figure out
if I'm more scared of being bound to this place
or being bound for someplace else

Names have been removed to protect identities

███ sped into ours when his was raided doors unlocked fuck the neighbourhood watch ███ thought sleeping bags could block the infrared from police helicopters hid a butter knife in there stashed it in his loft ████ took the *No* from the *Ball Games* sign badman dog shit on the playing field pick n mix for dinner you saw ██████ stuffing a sack of limbs into his boot finger to gold tooth *shush* you ever known anyone to call the feds ████ got sent inside came home to a ten pound baby gorgeous ██████ said that ██████ did that girl on the green but there was no body you said it was just a white rumour ███ & ███ & █████ & █ rinsed the care in the community flats ruthless we were fucking savage █████ ███ pumping his car stereo with that one tune every day that summer after you left heads know to look up when it plays

Bruv

At the funeral
the youngers swap spit
& sturdy kisses, snot
into each others armpits,
boys damp with the tender rage
of losing one of their own.
The older men expose
their fullness to the room
bare brick chests slicked in red stripe,
shove vodka cranberries & hot bagels
into my plump knuckled fists.
i am unprepared
for the softness of men.
i watch the neighbour boys drop
warm lumps of hash
onto the lowering coffin.
The uncle-geezers clutch
each other's hands in the battering sun.

in my mayonnaise half-life

i spent a year
washing

i held a rifle
clay pigeon
shooting with a gang
of toffs who said
they were hard

i used to be
a sister
he was 24
when i stopped

there were a few
times when I relaxed
my screwface
on the nightwalk
late-summer balm
had me all loose

dad once told me
i should have been
a wrestler
or a singer

*

once
my screwface sister gang
had me shooting
clay toffs

late-summer
they were spent
on a nightwalk
with a 24

held a year when
dad should have been
a balm or a rifle
he used
i stopped washing

there were a few times when
i said who i was
relaxed
the all of me

i pigeon singer
i loose wrestler
i told to be hard

*

a late-summer wrestler
once used me
had me on a rifle

be loose
he said
i spent 24 times
washing my screwface
with nightwalk balm
a few toffs were there
they were all a gang

should i have
told dad

i was a sister
a hard pigeon
who stopped the year
shooting clay

when held
to a singer
i relaxed

Names have been removed to protect identities (ii)

██ split his 99 flake with ██ popped him on his bikeseat backies
all summer foamy white drips on the handlebars ██ heaved his
nans blue bags after football you ever known anyone to call him soft
██ speeched the driver so the others could sneak past ████ with
his litany of how's your mum and dad are they alright yeh liberal with
his mate rates at the greengrocer ████ rescued a baby hedgehog
from the road scooped her up by her soft belly & passed her through
the fence gap precious parcel that she was we were fucking lovely
█████ handed out choc ices as if there were gold bars ████ put all
our doubles on his tab at the wake heads know to spill a little drink

The shadow of the tower, Notting Hill, Christmas 2016

Six months before it happens
I work a Christmas party,
cloakroom, top-ups, a bottle
to take home at the end
if I'm lucky. The blonde
so-and-so from such-and-such
news show blocks the church
opposite with her land rover,
can't you just tell the Vicar to fuck off.
In the crowd I notice
someone drowning
in a hot torrent of thankyous.
There she is amid the canapés, gagging
on all her terriblysorries
in front of all the staff,
as if apologising
for being alive,
when she was merely
handing over a cloakroom ticket.
Everyone in uniform
is awash with this small
drama but rescuing her from the perennial
humiliation of having everything done
for you is beyond
the job description.
All I can do is hand over
her coat with the solace of a doctor
delivering bad news.
I'm sorry madam
but all we can do
for you now is make
you as comfortable as possible.

i'd like for my closest people

to act like strangers
in the swimming pool changing rooms
diligently rubbing muffs dry
with bobbled towels
one leg up on the bench.
Or like strangers at the cinema
indulging in a good horror,
sharing the odd collective gasp
then exiting to separate bus stops.

i'd like to recover my teeth
from all the grinding,
retrieve my lost enamel dust
then fold it into slick-white
glue-dollops & newspaper
& make a tiny statue of myself
that i can hold in front of my face at parties.

The next time we see each other lets pretend
that we've met only once
& you can't remember my name
when you say my name
its like clingfilm
tight on my chunky drumsticks.

i want to multiply my own company
treat us all to a silent retreat in the Cotswolds
seperate bedrooms, all en-suite
really all i want is free
sanitary towels,
to lie on a soft carpet

in front of a screensaver
of a log fire,
give me one choice of moisturiser
a quiet stomach
the cartilage of a 12 year old boy
training for the local surf championships.

Autobiography Redacted

All she knows now is fear
& a hankering for meat.
Once, she slurped
a boy whole
in a phone booth.
It was New Year's.
There were fireworks.

Her skin hasn't aged
since she was six months old.
But her fruits
have been dried out
by men who never
go to work,
own houses & play
in multiple street bands.

She discovered
she didn't care
for anal.
Or seafood.
Or bank holidays.
Why not work through
the weekend & bunk off Monday.
Midday tinny in the park,
the whole place to yourself.

Acknowledgements

This pamphlet is called *Proverbs for a Woman Drinking Alone* but I am far from being solely responsible for this book. A huge thank you to Aaron Kent and the good people at Broken Sleep for welcoming me into the press. You are a beacon in this industry. Thank you to bath magg, The Interpreters House and Fenland Poetry Journey for publishing several of the poems in this pamphlet. I want to thank my friends in the Uni Slam Post Emerging Cohort for coaxing many of these poems out of me. The shared google doc during lockdown that we poured so much late-night attention into was truly a lifeline. I think you are all amazing. Thank you to Arts Council England for supporting my time to complete the manuscript. Shout out to my parents for *everything*. The grit and grace with which you move through the world, even at the hardest times is the greatest gift, the biggest lesson. I want to say sorry to my friends for the times I've flaked because I was busy writing, thank you for tolerating my chaos, I love you all to the ends of the earth. And finally, to my Jamie, I wish I could sum it up in a neat little sentence but I can't. All I can say is thank you for being you.

LAY OUT YOUR UNREST